# MAMMALS

GRACE JONES

Words that look like **this** can be found in the glossary on page 24.

©2018
The Secret Book
Company
King's Lynn
Norfolk PE30 4LS

ISBN: 978-1-912171-80-4

Written by:
Grace Jones

Designed by:
Ian McMullen

A catalogue record for this book
is available from the British Library

# contents

# What Are Living Things?

All living things move and grow. Living things need air, food, water and sunlight to stay alive.

**These are all living things.**

Frog

Tiger

Human

Knife, Fork and Plate

Books

**These are all non-living things.**

Non-living things do not move or grow. Non-living things do not need air, food, water or sunlight because they are not alive.

Teddy Bear

# What Is a Mammal?

Mammals a type of living thing that can live in water or on land. They need air, food, water and sunlight to live. Lions, dolphins and elephants are all mammals.

Elephant

**Fact: There are over 4,000 known species of mammal.**

Lion

Dolphin

Mammals breathe air. They usually have hair on their bodies and they all have a backbone. They are warm-blooded animals. This means that their body temperature does not change when the temperature does.

A polar bear stays warm even when it is freezing cold because it is warm-blooded.

# Where Do They Live?

Whales live in the ocean.

All living things live in a **habitat** or home. Mammals can live in many different habitats around the world. Some mammals

Other mammals live on land in the many deserts, mountains and forests and other land habitats that are found throughout the world.

A sloth in the rainforest.

# Mammal Homes

Some mammals, like mountain hairs, live under the ground in specially built homes called burrows. Their burrows provide them with shelter from **predators** and the cold weather.

A camel in
a desert in
Oman.

Other mammals, such as
camels, live in habitats
that have hotter **climates**
which get very little rain.
Camels have wide hooves
so they can walk on sand
easily without sinking
and can survive for many
months without water.

# What Do They Eat?

Adult mammals eat meat or plants, or a mixture of both. Some mammals that eat meat, like tigers, have long teeth, called canines, which help them to tear their **prey** into smaller pieces.

**Canines**

**Fact: Tigers are the largest of the big cats.**

Plant-eating animals, like cows, have wide, flat teeth to grind up grasses and grains.

13

# How Do They Breathe?

All mammals breathe in oxygen from the air through their lungs. Small mammals with little lungs breathe in and out very fast, while large animals breathe in and out slowly.

**Fact:**
A whale can stay under water for two hours without breathing.

**Blowhole**

Some mammals that live in water, like whales and dolphins, breathe in and out through nostrils on the top of their heads, called blowholes.

15

# How Do They Move?

The way mammals move depends on the habitat they live in. Mammals who live in the trees of rainforests will often have tails to help them balance and toes that they use to grip trees with.

Toes

Tail

Tarsier Monkey

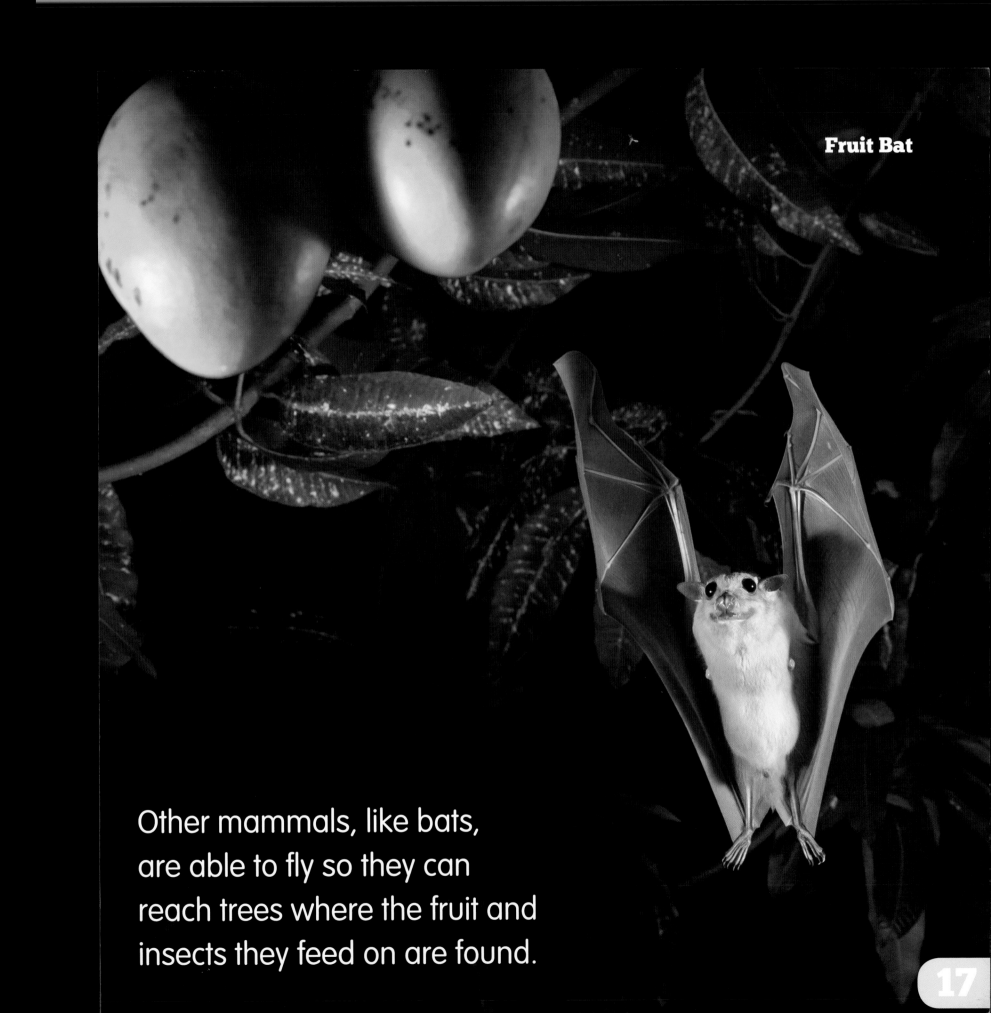

**Fruit Bat**

Other mammals, like bats, are able to fly so they can reach trees where the fruit and insects they feed on are found.

# How Do They Grow?

Most mammals start life as babies inside their mother's body before they are born. Some mammals have one baby and others have as many as fifteen.

The babies feed on their mother's milk whilst they are still growing and changing into an adult. This can take anywhere from a few months to many years.

# Marvellous Mammals

Mammals are the smartest animals in the world. The elephant has the largest brain of all mammals, including humans. They can still remember things that happened many years ago.

Mammals living in groups usually help each other out. Meerkats live in groups called colonies, which can include as many as 50 meerkats. They will normally have one babysitter who looks after the young when the other adults are looking for food.

# World Record Breakers

## BLUE WHALE

**Size:**
**Up to 30 metres long**

**Record:**
**World's Biggest Mammal**

**Fact:**
**The blue whale is the largest animal to have ever lived. Its tongue alone can weigh as much as an elephant!**

# GIRAFFE

**Record: World's Tallest Mammal**

**Size: Up to 6 metres long**

**Fact: Even baby giraffes are taller than most adult humans.**

# Glossary

**climates** types of weather in a particular place

**habitat** a home where animals and plants live

**nutrients** food needed for growth and health

**predators** any animal that eats other animals and insects

**prey** any animal or insect that is eaten by another

## Photo Credits

**Photocredits: Abbreviations: l-left, r-right, b-bottom, t-top, c-centre, m-middle. All images are courtesy of Shutterstock.com.**

Front Cover – ANP. 1,6r – Donovan van Staden. 2-3 – Eric Gevaert. 4bl – Chros. 4c – Eric Isselee. 4r – michaeljung. 5bl – Elena Schweitzer. 5tl – koosen. 5r – Lichtmeister. 6bl – Eric Isselee. 6bc – Willyam Bradberry. 7 – Tom linster. 8 – Seb c'est bien. 9 – nattanan726. 10 – Ng Yin Jian. 11 – Wolfgang Zwanzger. 12 – Michal Ninger. 13 – Dudarev Mikhail. 14 – Szasz-Fabian Jozsef. 15 – Christian Musat. 16 – Ondrej Prosicky. 17 – Ivan Kuzmin. 18 – Linn Currie. 19 – ryna Rasko. 20 – Custom media. 21 – tratong. 22 – powell'sPoint. 23 – E. O. 24 – ehtesham. Back Cover – Oleg Znamenskiy. All facts, statistics, web addresses and URLs in this book were verified as valid and accurate at time of writing. No responsibility for any changes to external websites or references can be accepted by either the author or publisher.